The Nitty-gritty of Family Life

A Children's Book about Living in a Family

by

Joy Wilt

Illustrated by Ernie Hergenroeder

Educational Products Division
Word, Incorporated
Waco, Texas

Author

JOY WILT is creator and director of Children's Ministries, an organization that provides resources "for people who care about children"—speakers, workshops, demonstrations, consulting services, and training institutes. A certified elementary school teacher, administrator, and early childhood specialist, Joy is also consultant to and professor in the master's degree program in children's ministries for Fuller Theological Seminary. Joy is a graduate of LaVerne College, LaVerne, California (B.A. in Biological Science), and Pacific Oaks College, Pasadena, California (M.A. in Human Development). She is author of three books, *Happily Ever After, An Uncomplicated Guide to Becoming a Superparent,* and *Taming the Big Bad Wolves,* as well as the popular *Can-Make-And-Do Books.* Joy's commitment "never to forget what it feels like to be a child" permeates the many innovative programs she has developed and her work as lecturer, consultant, writer, and—not least—mother of two children, Christopher and Lisa.

Artist

ERNIE HERGENROEDER is founder and owner of Hergie & Associates (a visual communications studio and advertising agency). With the establishment of this company in 1975, "Hergie" and his wife, Faith, settled in San Jose with their four children, Lynn, Kathy, Stephen, and Beth. Active in community and church affairs, Hergie is involved in presenting creative workshops for teachers, ministers, and others who wish to understand the techniques of communicating visually. He also lectures in high schools to encourage young artists toward a career in commercial art. Hergie serves as a consultant to organizations such as the Police Athletic League (PAL), Girl Scouts, and religious and secular corporations. His ultimate goal is to touch the hearts of kids (8 to 80) all over the world—visually!

Contents

Introduction

<u>The Nitty-gritty of Family Life</u> is one of a series of books.   The complete set is called *Ready-Set-Grow!*

<u>The Nitty-gritty of Family Life</u> deals with the child as a member of a family and can be used by itself or as part of a program that utilizes all of the *Ready-Set-Grow!* books.

<u>The Nitty-gritty of Family Life</u> is specifically designed so that children can either read the book themselves or have it read to them. This can be done at home, church, or school. When reading to children, it is not necessary to complete the book at one sitting. Concern should be given to the attention span of the individual child and his or her comprehension of the subject matter.

<u>The Nitty-gritty of Family Life</u> is designed to involve the child in the concepts that are being taught. This is done by simply and carefully explaining each concept and then asking questions that invite a response from the child. It is hoped that by answering the questions the child will personalize the concept and, thus, integrate it into his or her thinking.

The Nitty-gritty of Family Life defines the word family as "a group of people (two or more) who are related to each other and share the same home." The book helps the child understand his or her role as a member of a family.

Family relationships, rules, and responsibilities are all a part of family life.   The Nitty-gritty of Family Life gives the following guidelines:

> establish healthy relationships with other family members,
>
> accept rules as a vital part of family life, and
>
> share responsibilities (if family life is to run smoothly, every family member must do his or her part.)

The Nitty-gritty of Family Life is designed to give the child a better understanding of his or her role as member of a family. This book is also designed to teach a child that everything God does has a purpose and fits into a total plan. "Family life" is a part of God's plan. Children who grow up believing and accepting this will be better equipped to live healthy, exciting lives.

The Nitty-gritty of Family Life

It is part of God's plan for you that you are a part of a family.

Your family is special, just as every other family is special.

No two families are exactly alike.
Every family is different.

Families come in different colors.

Families come in different sizes.

Some families are small.

Some families are large.

Families come in different ages.

Some families are young.

Some families are old.

This is a family.

This is a family.

This is a family.

This is a family.

This is a family.

A family is two or more people who are related to each other and often share the same home.

Some families live in houses.

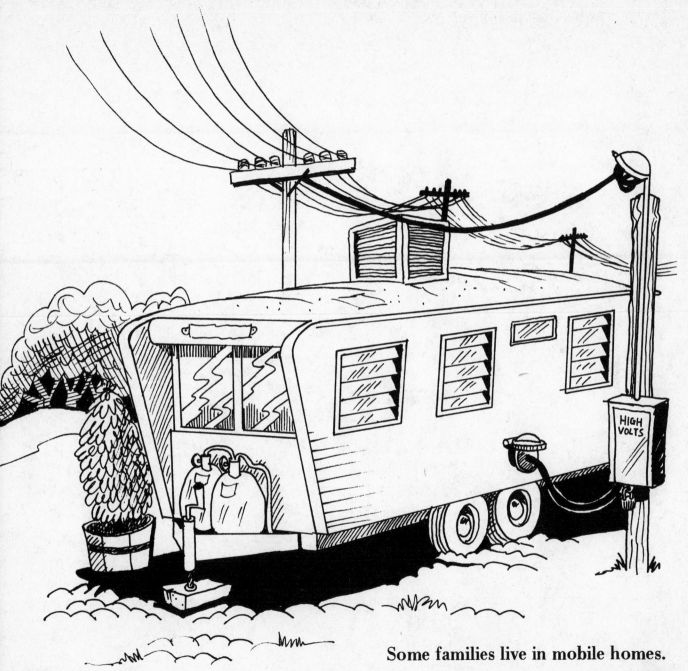

Some families live in mobile homes.

Some families live in apartments.

Some families live on farms.

What is your family like?

How many people are in your family?

There are four peopel

What are their names and ages?

Neige 8 Joey 12 Dad 38 mom 37

Where does your family live?

My famaly lives in a condomimnin

Chapter 1

Family Roles

When a man has or adopts a child, he becomes a father.

When a woman has or adopts a child, she becomes a mother.

Every boy is his father and mother's son.

If there are other children in a boy's family, he is their brother.

Every girl is her father and mother's daughter.

If there are other children in a girl's family, she is their sister.

A father's father is a grandfather.

A father's mother is a grandmother.

A mother's father is a grandfather.

A mother's mother is a grandmother.

THIS IS MY MOTHER.

THIS IS OUR GRANDMOTHER JONES.

A father's brother is an uncle.

A father's sister is an aunt.

A mother's brother is an uncle.

A mother's sister is an aunt.

An uncle and aunt's children are cousins.

THESE ARE OUR CHILDREN.

THESE ARE OUR COUSINS.

Father, mother, brother(s), and sister(s)
are called the immediate family.

Grandparents, uncles, aunts, and cousins are called the extended family.

Who is in your immediate family?

Neige, Mom Dad Joey

Who is in your extended family?

Are you a brother? ✗ Y

Are you a sister? ✓

Are you an uncle? ✗

Are you an aunt? ✗

Are you a cousin? ✓

Chapter 2

Family Relationships

When two people are around each other a lot, they
sometimes have disagreements and fights.

Sometimes a mother and father disagree and fight with each other.

Sometimes a parent and child disagree and fight with each other.

Sometimes a child disagrees and fights with a brother or sister.

It is normal for people who are together a lot to have disagreements and fights.

Disagreements and fights can often be good.

They can allow people to express their anger, frustration, and other feelings that may be upsetting them.

They can allow people to get problems out in the open and hopefully solve them.

Family disagreements and fights can often be helpful if family members remember these three things.

Family members should be honest with each other. They should tell each other the truth about what is happening, and what they think and feel about the situation.

Family members should not harm each other.

Family members should love, respect, and trust each other.

Family disagreements and fights are an important part of family relationships.

Cooperation is also an important part of family relationships.

It is very important that family members cooperate and help each other learn and grow.

Support is also an important part of family relationships.

61

It is very important that family members support each other when someone needs help.

Sharing is also an important part of family relationships.

It is very important that family members share their
things with each other.

Remember.

Family disagreements and fights can often be helpful if family members

>   are honest with each other;
>
>   do not harm each other; and
>
>   love, respect, and trust each other.

Family relationships will be better if family members

cooperate with each other,

support each other, and

share with each other.

How are your relationships with the people in your family?

When you disagree and fight, are you honest? ☑ ☐
                                                     Yes No

Do you try not to harm each other? ☑ ☐
                                       Yes No

Do you love, respect, and trust each other? ☑ ☐
                                                Yes No

Do you cooperate with the people in your family? ☑ ☐
                                                       Yes No

Do you support them? ☑ ☐
                     Yes No

Do you share your things with them? ☑ ☐
                                        Yes NO

Chapter 3

Family Rules

Wherever there are two or more people, it is important to have rules.

Rules are guidelines that tell people how to act and what to do.

Every family has rules. Some rules are talked about and agreed upon by everyone in the family. These are called spoken rules. Here is an example of a spoken rule.

Other rules may not be talked about and agreed upon, but everyone in the family knows that they exist. These rules are called unspoken rules. Here is an example of an unspoken rule.

I'D SURE LIKE TO HAVE SOME OF THAT CAKE. MOM DIDN'T SAY I COULDN'T... BUT I BETTER NOT TAKE A PIECE, BECAUSE SHE DIDN'T SAY THAT I COULD. MAYBE SHE BAKED IT FOR SOMETHING SPECIAL.

Spoken rules are oftentimes more effective than unspoken ones. When a spoken rule is made, everyone has a chance to talk about the rule and make sure he or she understands it. But when a rule is not talked over by the family members, sometimes it can be misunderstood. Whether a rule is spoken or unspoken, it needs to be respected and followed equally by every member of the family.

Because every family is different, every family has a different set of rules. Each family must make a set of rules that fits its particular situation.

When a family makes a set of rules, it should be remembered that rules work best when everyone who has to obey them helps make the rules.

It is important for families to have rules about space.

Rules about space tell family members

what areas in and around the home are OK to be in,

what areas in and around the home are off limits,

what activities can and cannot be done in certain areas, and

where family members can and cannot go when they leave home.

What are your family's rules about space?

What areas in and around your home are OK for you to be in?

Madagan Villedg R.M.S.'s park

What areas in and around your home are off limits to you?

34 6 Jorgan Vilage, Marks, way
out in the city

In what areas are you allowed to eat?

kitchen, living room, out side   sometimes

Are there any areas where you are not allowed to eat?

Living room, Bedrooms, famly room

In what areas are you allowed to make a mess?

Kitchen tabbel or conter

Are there any areas where you are not allowed to make a mess?

Bedrooms, livingroom, famly room, bathroom, kitchen

In what areas can you play?

Bedrooms, livingroom, famlyroom Basment, kitchen, outside

Are there any areas where you are not allowed to play?

far away moms and dads room

Where are you allowed to go when you leave home?

School, freds house, park

Are there any places you aren't allowed to go?

Mac's, stor, strangeris house, far away

It is important for families to have rules about time.

Rules about time tell family members

when things happen (the family schedule),

when certain things should be finished, and

when things can and cannot be done at certain times.

What are your family rules about time?

Do you have special times when you eat your meals? ☑ ☐
                                                        Yes No

When do you eat breakfast? morning 8:05

When do you eat lunch? afternoon 12:00

When do you eat dinner? evning 6:00

When do you have to be home in the evening? 5:15 I don't know

When is your bedtime? 8o'clook

Are there other times when you or your family do certain things? ☑ Yes ☐ No

**If there are, use this chart to list some of
those times and what activities are done then.**

TIME	ACTIVITY
Sunday	go to Church
Saterday	fun things
Friday	Go out to Mantis
Cristmis	Go out to the farm

It is important for families to have rules about possessions.

Rules about possessions tell family members

what each person owns,

what owners can and cannot do with their things,

how to borrow and return things, and

what must be done when someone's things are lost, abused, or broken by another family member.

What are your family's rules about possessions?

What are some of the things you own?

toys, close, dreser, closet, shelf, tabel, books,
food
blankets, stickers, hats, math cards, pensels, erasers
pensel sharpaner

What are you allowed to do with the things you own?

play with them, if its close Im alod to where it
I can use it

What are you not allowed to do with the things you own?

brack them, throw them, stp on them, rip them

If you want to borrow something from another family member, what do you have to do?

Take care of them.

If someone should lose, abuse, or break your things, what would happen?

They would get in trobel if it was my family member

If you should lose, abuse, or break someone else's things, what would happen?

I would get in trobel

It is important for families to have rules about work.

Rules about work tell family members

     who is supposed to work,

     what work needs to be done,

     when the work needs to be done, and

     where the work needs to be done.

FAMILY WORK CHART

Name	Job to be done	When the job is to be done
Bill *anyperson* *meorjoey* *Dad or mon* *me* *everyone* *everyone* *nodne* *mom* *me Joey mom Dad* *me or* *JOey*	Empty the trash	Every Tuesday and Thursday
	Dry the dishes	Every other week
	Set the table	Every other week
	Make his bed and clean his room	Every day
	Mow the lawn and weed the garden	Every other Saturday
	Vacuum and dust the house	Every other Saturday
Mary *me or Joey, or dad or mom* *me Joey mom Dad mom me, dad* *mom*	Feed the dog and cat	Every day
	Dry the dishes	Every other week
	Set the table	Every other week
	Make her bed and clean her room	Every day
	Mow the lawn and weed the garden	Every other Saturday
	Vacuum and dust the house	Every other Saturday

89

What are your family's rules about work?

Make a work chart for your family.

	FAMILY
Name	**Job to be done**
MOM dad Neige Joey	clean disis Vacum clean the mess go to work make the bathroom make my bed clean my room eqt make his bed clean his room

90

WORK CHART

When the job is to be done

It is important for families to have rules about play.

Rules about play tell family members

who is OK to play with,

what is healthy and safe to play with,

when it is healthy and safe to play, and

where it is healthy and safe to play.

What are your family's rules about play?

Who are some of the people it is good for you to play with?

Amy, Carla, Chelsy, Jamie, Malissa, Dean, tim
Candic

Who are some of the people you shouldn't play with?

Serna, Jhon,

What are some of the things that are healthy and safe to play with?

teddy Bar, My Cat, My Barbys, My Freinds

What are some of the things you shouldn't play with?

_____

When is it healthy and safe for you to play?

_____

When shouldn't you play?

_____

Where is it healthy and safe for you to play?

_____

Where shouldn't you play?

_____

It is important for families to have rules about habits and customs.

Rules about habits and customs tell family members

what they will do during time spent together;

what they will do for vacations, holidays, and special events;

how often certain practices will be repeated; and

how the family will choose to act or behave.

What are your family's rules about habits and customs?

Did your family have a vacation together this year? ☑ ☒
Yes   No

What did you do?

go to ~~school~~ Marable

List some of the holidays your family celebrates together.

Christmas

Birthdays

List other special events that happen in your family.

Cristmas   camping

Birthdays

Does your whole family ever get together during the day? ☑ Yes ☐ No

If so, what does your family do then?

_____eat go bike rideing_____

Are there special times set aside when your family does certain things? ☑ Yes ☐ No

List some things your family chooses to do again and again.

_____

_____

It is important for families to have rules.

Some rules are spoken while others are unspoken.

Whether a rule is spoken or unspoken, it is important that it be respected and followed by every member of the family.

Every family has its own set of rules about

      space,
      time,
      possessions,
      work,
      play, and
      habits and customs.

Chapter 4

Family Responsibilities

Wherever there are two or more people, there are always jobs that have to be done.

Jobs are often called responsibilities.

103

It is not fair for one person in any family to take all of the responsibility and do every job that needs to be done. It is not good for the person who is doing everything, and it is not good for the people who are letting that person do everything.

If a family is to be healthy and happy, everyone must take some responsibility. Everyone must work so that no one person is doing everything.

Food, clothes, and a place to live cost money.

Someone has to earn money for the family to use.

All the things that a family uses need to be purchased.

Someone has to shop for the things that the family needs.

Things that the family buys must be paid for.

Someone has to pay the money that the family owes.

In order to live, people in the family need to eat.

Someone has to prepare the food for the family to eat.

When people live in a home, it gets dirty and messy.

Someone has to organize and clean the place where the family lives.

When people wear clothing, it gets dirty too.
Someone has to wash and dry the clothes that the family wears.

111

Things that are used by the family sometimes break or stop working.
Someone has to repair the things that break or stop working.

Some families live in homes where there are jobs to be done outside.

Someone has to do the work on the lawn and the outside of the house to keep them in good shape.

Some families own a car.

Someone has to clean, wash, and take care of the car.

There are babies and/or young children in some families.

Someone has to take care of the babies and small children in a family.

Some families have a pet.

Someone has to take care of the family pet.

Wherever there are families, there will always be garbage and trash.

Someone has to take care of the garbage and trash.

These are just a few of the responsibilities that families have. In every family there are a lot of jobs that need to be done.

A family can be healthy and happy if everyone remembers these two things.

Family members should always try to "share the load." Each person should take some responsibility and do his or her part to help the family out.

Family members should always try to appreciate one another for the things each person does.

Who earns the money that your family uses?

_____ mom and dad _____

Who shops for the things that your family needs?

_____ mom and dad _____

Who pays the money that your family owes? (Who pays the bills?)

_____ mom and dad _____

Who prepares the food that your family eats?

_____ mom and dad _____

Who organizes and cleans the place where your family lives?

_____ me Joey mom and dad _____

Who washes and dries the clothes that your family wears?

_____ mom _____

Who repairs the things that break or stop working?

_____ dad _____

Who does the work on the lawn and the outside of the house?

no won

Who cleans, washes, and takes care of the car?

dad

Who takes care of the babies and small children in your family?

mom ahd dad

Who takes care of your family's pet?

me mom dad and joey

Who takes care of the garbage and trash?

evry one

What are some of your responsibilities? What are some of the jobs you do to help your family? _lots ov thing_

Do you remember to appreciate and say thank-you to the other people in your family who are doing things to help out? ☑ ☐
Yes   No

120

Conclusion

It is true that families do not stay the same forever.

Sometimes new members are added to families.

Children grow up and move away. **123**

People grow old and die.

But families go on and on.

As long as there are people, there will be families:

Families where people laugh, cry, work, play, and grow together;
Families where people fight and then make up;
Families where people share and help each other out.

Being part of a family isn't always easy. There are

        roles that have to be fulfilled,
        relationships that have to be developed,
        rules that have to be obeyed, and
        responsibilities that have to be done.

But that's what life is all about. These things are all a part of living, growing, and . . .

The nitty-gritty of family life